Let's Have a
Party!

Also by Honey and Larry Zisman

The 47 Best Chocolate Chip Cookies in the World
57 More of the Best Chocolate Chip Cookies in the World
The Great American Peanut Butter Book
The Burger Book
The 50 Best Cheesecakes in the World
The 50 Best Oatmeal Cookies in the World
The 55 Best Brownies in the World
Super Sweets
The Great International Dessert Cookbook
Chocolate Fantasies
The Ultimate Lunchbox Book

St. Martin's Griffin

New York

Let's Have a Party!

The Winning Entries in the Nationwide
Children's Birthday Party Contest

Honey & Larry Zisman and Jordana LeBlanc

Designed by Bryanna Millis

Library of Congress Cataloging-in-Publication Data

Zisman, Honey.
    Let's have a party! : the winning entries in the nationwide
  Children's Birthday Party Contest / Honey Zisman, Larry Zisman,
  Jordana LeBlanc. — 1st St. Martin's Griffin ed.
        p.   cm.
    ISBN 0-312-18126-4
    1. Children's parties.   2. Birthdays.   I. Zisman, Larry.
  II. LeBlanc, Jordana.   III. Title.
  GV1205.Z57   1998
  793.2'1—dc21   97-31755
                                                                            CIP

First St. Martin's Griffin Edition: February 1998

10   9   8   7   6   5   4   3   2   1

For
Jackie, Craig, and Corina Rose

❀   ❀   ❀

May every day of their lives be
as joyful as a great party

❀ Contents ❀

Let's Have a Party!
  It will be great fun,
Much enjoyment when it's happening,
  Fond memories when it's done.

Let's Have a Party!

1

Joy and Enjoyment, Not Fear and Fright

❀   ❀   ❀   ❀   ❀   ❀   ❀

For some people it is the hype and spectacle of the Super Bowl. For others, it is the suspense and glamor of the Academy Awards. And many look forward to the frantic celebrating and the promises of a new beginning on New Year's Eve.

But for children, their birthdays are the main event of the year. They anticipate not only becoming a year older, moving closer to being a grown-up, but of course having a great birthday party.

For some parents, though, a birthday party can seem like a nightmare: fifteen hungry and energetic kids running through the house, with nothing to feed them or to amuse them, much less to get them to celebrate the anniversary of your son's or daughter's birth.

Relax!

Wake up relieved because help is right at hand within the pages of this book.

In *Let's Have a Party!* you will find more birthday party themes than you will ever need. Additional tips and suggestions will ensure a smoothly run and thoroughly enjoyable party not only for the birthday child and the guests but also for the parents who attend. Most importantly, *you* will find enough guidance to plan and prepare a memorable party so that you can have a good time yourself. After the party is over, you will be able to say honestly, "It was really fun . . . I can't wait until next year!"

Collected here are the winning entries in the LET'S HAVE A PARTY! contest, gathered from across the United States from parents just like you, who have succeeded in planning and throwing terrific birthday parties. They share them here so that children and parents everywhere can celebrate and enjoy the child's special day.

❀ **Where Else Can We Have the Party?** ❀

Besides your own living room, family room, basement, or backyard, there are many, many places outside the home that offer a special setting for a very entertaining birthday party. Don't forget the obvious advantage of not having to clean up after everyone has gone home.

Going out for a party for older children—ten- to twelve-year-olds—is a particularly good idea, since it makes the party a little more "grown-up" and different from the usual cake and ice-cream parties that little kids have at home.

Every city and town has its own fun sites to hold a party. All you have to do is a little research, talk to a few friends, and make some telephone calls and you should be able to find just the right place to celebrate your son's or daughter's birthday in style . . . and make it a memorable day for everyone.

Here are some locations that you might want to consider for your party. Remember, this is only a suggested listing, and you probably can find other enjoyable places right around where you live:

- a community room at the library
- an indoor playground
- a video arcade
- museums: including art museums, science museums, natural history museums, local history museums, agricultural museums
- a water slide activity park
- a community swimming pool or swim club
- the seashore (beach, ocean, and boardwalk)
- a gymnastics center
- a laser game playland
- arts and crafts stores
- a beauty salon
- a farm
- tennis or basketball courts
- a college student center
- a movie theater
- a local stage show
- amusement parks or piers
- hotels
- catering halls
- a community recreation center
- restaurants
- a tearoom
- an ice-cream parlor
- a park
- a hiking trail
- a wildlife park
- a church hall
- a charter boat
- a sight-seeing train
- an airport

4

- a nature center
- a zoo
- an aquarium
- a miniature golf course

The list of possible places is really endless, limited only by what is available in your area, the activities you want to have at the party, and the cost of using the facility.

❀ What Kind of Entertainment Can We Have for the Party? ❀

There are many different kinds of entertainment to have at your party depending on the age of the children attending, the place where the party is being held, the theme of the party, and, of course, how much money you want to spend.

It is important to get several recommendations from others who have had the same entertainment you are considering, hold auditions yourself, or go see the people you might hire when they are performing elsewhere. This advance preparation will let you know exactly what you will be getting so there will be no unpleasant surprises at your own party.

Ideas for having party entertainment include:

- a magician (an adult who is a professional or a talented high school student)
- a clown (one who does face painting, nail painting, and balloon sculpture as well as putting on a show)
- pony rides

- a traveling petting zoo
- a park ranger who brings unusual animals
- a "cowboy"
- musicians
- folksingers
- a storyteller

- a puppet show
- a mime
- people in the costumes of cartoon characters, superheros, or television show characters like Barney
- local athletes
- a local television personality

- a science show
- an acting troupe
- a gymnastics group
- an inflatable jumping playground
- a traveling tumbling gym
- an arts and crafts instructor
- a cooking instructor

Since what can go wrong frequently does, be prepared with alternative activities in case your entertainment fails to arrive or if the party guests, for whatever reasons, show no interest in the planned program or activities.

The key to planning and having a successful birthday party for your child is to follow several essential guidelines.

- Most importantly, think about your son's or daughter's personality when deciding what kind of party to have. Is she outgoing, gregarious, and does she love to be the center of attention? If so, a large party with her as the queen and her friends as ladies-in-waiting would be just right.

On the other hand, if your son is the shy, reserved type it would be better to have a small group of just three or four friends for the party. The noise level stays down, and he will not feel overwhelmed by having too many people crowding around him. It will be a comfortable situation that he can handle.

• If you are having a party for a young preschooler who is afraid of strangers or of large dress-up figures like Santa and the Easter Bunny at the mall, don't hire a TV character to come to the party no matter how much they like a particular program. Remember, television characters are seen on a comparatively small screen. Children are used to seeing a small Barney, a small Mickey Mouse, or a small Winnie-the-Pooh, and they will not be prepared for the monstrous figures who show up at your door, not sounding like the familiar friends from television or not talking at all.

• Regardless of how elaborate or how simple the party will be, do not over-organize or overorchestrate. If you are the type who likes to plan and control everything down to the smallest detail, that's fine, but be prepared for some of your hard work to go unused or change as the party progresses. Few children's parties ever go exactly as they are planned.

Children don't like to get bogged down in detailed instructions for activities. Keep in mind that it's not just one child you are dealing with, but, rather, it's a whole group. And it's not school; it's play, and it should be easy and fun. If there is too much explaining of games or other activities, the kids will become bored; even the older children have enough of organization in school and will want fewer rules and more spontaneity.

• Parties are supposed to be fun for everyone, the people running them as well as all the guests. Know your own limitations in hosting a party. If having a dozen children over for three hours will be too much commotion and too big a project for you, consider scaling it down and having half as many guests for two hours. It is better to have fewer people and less fuss than turn into a screaming ogre when things get out of hand with a larger group.

• A few words about decorations are in order. Decorations really add to the festivities. They can put everyone in the mood for whatever type of party you are having. Imagine coming into a home and seeing colorful, cutout fish floating from strings attached to the ceiling, hula skirts tossed over chair backs, large colorful posters of tropical islands, and having flower leis hung around your neck as you enter. Immediately you are transported to another place, another world, far from where you were before you came inside.

There isn't any party, no matter what the theme, that would not be enhanced and made more enjoyable by the right trimmings. But don't feel that decorations have to be elaborate either. Large bundles of easy-to-blow-up balloons are enough to say: Welcome to the festivities!

A small word of caution: think about the age of the participants when decorating to make sure that the decorations are age appropriate. For instance, balloons should be tied up, out of the reach of tiny hands. The floor should be kept as free of clutter as possible. If something like cutout footprints are to stay on the floor, they should be securely taped down. Decorations that sit right on the floor are better set up in an out-of-the-way niche or in a corner, well away from scampering feet.

• Now let's talk about those take-home bribes—also known as "goodie bags." Goodie bags are usually given as an enticement to the guests to get them to leave the party and go home. Even though you probably will not see the bags

A Special Note

Although latex balloons have long been an almost essential part of birthday party decorations, parents should be aware that there is a real hazard that younger children—from about eight years old and under—could choke on balloons.

Choking occurs when children inhale balloons while trying to inflate them or swallow pieces of broken balloons.

A safer alternative would be shiny foil (Mylar) balloons. These are far less risky because they are easier to inflate and less likely to be inhaled. They do not explode into small pieces that can be swallowed; and if they are swallowed, they do not restrict the breathing passages the way latex does.

opened and the articles inside used, the last remembrance of your fabulous party will be that special gift.

Beware of cheap, thin plastic doodads that look cute but are under contract to break just as soon as a child takes a look at them. The toys in the goodie bag are actually extensions of your party and your home and, therefore, should be chosen with thought, pride, and creativity.

- Although ice cream and cake are viewed as the absolute and irreplaceable party dessert, it is not written in stone that you must have them. There are good alternatives for everything, even the sacred ice cream and cake. Try cupcakes for a change, or petit fours or fancy muffins with icing. Instead of ice cream, have pudding: vanilla or chocolate or even rice pudding or tapioca. How about sherbet? Rainbow sherbet with its mixture of flavors is especially attractive, and healthier, too. Chances are, if it is sweet, kids will eat it and enjoy it.
- Here is a final tip when planning your party: *make lists*. Make lists for everything: a list of children you are inviting, a list of foods to be served, a list of

decorations, a list of toys to buy for grab bags or goodie bags or prizes. Get the idea?

Set up a special place in the house to keep all your lists and the things you buy for the party. As you complete each item on a list, mark it off with a bold crayon or felt tip pen. No one can remember all the party details in his head, so it pays to have and refer to as many lists as you need.

HAPPY BIRTHDAY, EVERYONE

2

Child-Proven Party Themes

❀   ❀   ❀   ❀   ❀   ❀   ❀

The Winning Entries in the LET'S HAVE A PARTY! Contest

It is not easy to keep a house full of boys and girls interested and entertained, even if they are excited about being at a birthday party for one of their friends.

It takes more than just cake and ice cream to make a successful and enjoyable afternoon, and the winning entries in the LET'S HAVE A PARTY! contest offer plenty of great ways to make a bunch of children say, "Wow, I had a great time! I can't wait for her birthday next year."

Remember, though, like all good ideas, the party themes here are only suggestions. Consider them starting points to be modified or expanded upon, rather than absolute blueprints for the parties you plan for your children. Every party theme here can be adapted so that your child's special party is an exact fit and makes your son or daughter and all the guests happy.

Use your imagination and think of all the people, places, and things where you live and how they can be brought together to create your own memorable event after someone very important to you says:

"MY BIRTHDAY IS COMING, LET'S HAVE A PARTY!"

❀ Garden Party ❀

Bridget E. Greene
Woodland Hills, California

Age Group: Three to six years old

Invitations: Flowerpot invitations sent along with flower seeds

Special Theme Food: Box lunches, food "Trade Me" box, "dirt" cake

Decorations: Handmade flowers that are similar to the invitations and hung around the party room

Activities: Paste the Flower on the Stem, planting an herb, water target game

Goodie Bag: Game prizes, potted herb, garden tool set, garden-related toys and candies

❀   ❀   ❀   ❀   ❀

Here's What to Do: We had a Garden Party to celebrate my daughter's third birthday. My daughter and I did most of the preparations together, which was more than half the fun.

We invited only six children to the party, since this idea works best with a small number.

Our invitations were handmade. We colored a drawing of a planter with stems sticking out. The number "3" was cut out from several different brightly colored sheets of construction paper and pasted onto the stems so it looked like a sprouting pot of 3-shaped "flowers." We then added glitter and paper grass. The invitations were sent out in large, bright orange mailing envelopes covered with insect and flower stickers to carry out the garden theme.

For the food we made box lunches, each one labeled with a guest's name. Each box had a piece of bologna, half a peanut butter and jelly sandwich, half a butter-and-pickle sandwich, a small bag of chips, individually wrapped string cheese or yellow cheese, grapes, and lemonade.

There was a food "Trade Me" box that had a little bit of everything in it. I encouraged the guests to trade with me or with their friends if there were some food they didn't like or would rather have. The "Trade Me" box was a definite hit, as was lunch. You can tailor the food choices to what your kids like.

The adults had sub sandwiches from a local sub shop along with lemonade and potato chips.

Our first activity was Paste the Flower on the Stem, our party's version of Pin the Tail on the Donkey. We copied the planter drawing used on the invitation on poster board,

Kiddie Cover-ups

Have a selection of large old shirts or T-shirts for the children to wear as cover-ups over their party clothes if the activities at the party will include something dirty or messy, such as finger painting or planting new flowers. There will be less mess for you after the painting and planting is done and no parents upset because their children came home from the party with dirty clothes.

making it larger, of course. Then we made construction paper flowers big enough for three-year-olds to handle for pasting up on the board. Each guest was blindfolded in turn and got a chance to try and paste a flower on a stem. The one closest to the stem received a prize.

Another fun activity was picking out and planting a small herb. Each guest got a little plastic pot and saucer marked with his or her name, a small bucket, and an inexpensive three-piece garden tool set of a rake, a shovel, and a hoe. We had filled a wagon with potting soil and small herb plants. The herb plants were different shapes and colors, and it was fun for the kids to choose which one to plant. The children needed very little help to plant their herbs. They had a ball.

It was a hot day in May when we had this party so we also played an outdoor game with a hose. The guests had been told to bring swimsuits. We put large soda bottles filled with varying amounts of water on top of a sawhorse and everyone tried to knock the bottles off using the stream from a hose. Prizes were awarded. It was a hit—there were no losers in this game—we all got wet and had a great time.

Prizes for the games were microscope pens, flying whirly butterflies, and big plastic insects.

There was a "dirt cake" for the birthday finale. Prepared in an authentic garden pot, it consisted of crushed Oreo cookies, whipped cream, and Gummi worms. Sprinkle a layer of crushed cookies on top to look like dirt. We served the "cake" with a shovel into paper bowls. It was rich.

For the take-home party favors, the guests got a brown bag with some goodies: Gummi worms, jelly candies in the shape of bugs, bug stickers, and a bug catcher box with a plastic bug in it for starters. Any garden-related item will also do. They also took home their garden tool set, their bucket, and their planted herb.

❀   ❀   ❀   ❀   ❀

Let's Have More Fun! Include a pack of flower, vegetable, or herb seeds with the invitation to add to the garden motif of the party.

Hang up hand-drawn flowers similar to the ones used in Paste the Stem on the Flower around the party room to add to the decor.

❀ **Fisherman's Party** ❀

Avis Langlois

Essex Junction, Vermont

Age Group: Six to nine years old

Invitations: Fish or fat worm invitations

Special Theme Food: Fish punch, pretzel fishing rods, "bait cups"

Decorations: Fishing gear and inflatable fish

Activities: Fish stories, fish puzzle

Goodie Bag: Books about fish and fishing

❀   ❀   ❀   ❀   ❀

Here's What to Do: Here is an idea that my parents would do when we lived in North Carolina near the ocean. We had a Fisherman's Party for both boys and girls, since just about everyone back there enjoyed fishing.

It was easy to decorate the house, since we had the fishing rods and reels and bait boxes and other kinds of fishing equipment. We also had large inflatable fish as decorations. For food we bought bait cups from a bait shop and filled them with M&M's, pretzels, mints, and other candies. In other cups we put licorice pieces cut to look like worms and pieces of Jell-O cut to look like small pieces of bait fish. This part was a little creepy, but the kids loved it. We also tied long string licorice to the ends of long pretzel sticks so they looked like fishing poles. Fish-shaped crackers were stuck to the end of the licorice strings. The cake was shaped like a big fish with the inscription "This birthday is one that didn't get away." We called the punch—just a mixture of fruit juices and ginger ale—"fish juice," and there were some plastic fish floating around in it.

We told "the biggest fish" stories and also created a group fish story. One person started the story and then we went around in a circle as each person added to the story. There were some rather strange fish in those stories.

The party favors for the guests when they left were books on fish and fishing, geared to the ages of the children who came to the party.

❀　　❀　　❀　　❀　　❀

Let's Have More Fun! Make invitations out of light blue construction paper. Cut the paper into fish and fat worm shapes. Write all the information in black ink.

Sprinkle candies shaped like fish, worms, and other yucky bait creatures all over the table.

Preparing for Good Party Manners

Kids are honest and say what they think, sometimes whatever pops into their mind, without realizing how it affects someone else. Remember this candor when the presents are being opened and someone shouts, "I have that and I broke it because it stinks!" Be prepared to have a comforting reply so the person who gave that present will not feel badly.

Another possibility is that your son or daughter already has a toy or game given as a gift and announces that fact in a loud and disappointed voice. A preparty etiquette talk might be helpful so something hurtful is not blurted out.

Also keep in mind that some presents will be less expensive than others, and talk to your child about being gracious for everything he or she gets.

—Adrian James
Manchester, New Hampshire

If you don't have fishing equipment around the house, you can cut out fish shapes from construction paper, or hang up pictures of ocean and harbor scenes that you draw or clip from a magazine.

Draw a large fish on a piece of light cardboard and color it. Cut the picture of the fish into large uneven puzzle pieces, enough pieces so that each guest gets at least one. Then have the children put the fish puzzle back together as quickly as possible, timing several tries to see how fast they can "catch the fish."

❀ Paint Party ❀

Maxine Palmer
Boise, Idaho

Age Group: Two to twelve years old
Invitations: Painting by birthday boy or girl on plain white paper, with information written on top
Special Theme Food: Bowls of Jell-O in different colors
Decorations: Homemade pictures of paintbrushes
Activities: Painting pictures, T-shirts, and cookies
Goodie Bag: Painted T-shirts, framed pictures, paintbrushes, paints, paper

❀　　　❀　　　❀　　　❀　　　❀

Here's What to Do: Here's a party idea that keeps kids of varying ages happy and occupied during the party as well as gives them something to take home when they leave. Have painting be the focus of the day.

The equipment needed is inexpensive and readily available. Get several sets of watercolor paints, a bunch of paintbrushes of varying sizes and shapes, canvases or pads of watercolor paper, and plastic cups for holding water to use with the paints. Have on hand old shirts or aprons that the kids can wear over their clothes to keep them clean.

Cover a table or floor space with plastic tablecloths or drop cloths for extra protection.

Buy a number of inexpensive frames, enough to have at least one for every child at the party. Each guest chooses his or her favorite picture and gets to frame it. You could also give out prizes for "Most Colorful," "Most Creative," and so on.

The extra paints can be taken home by the guests as they leave, along with their framed picture.

❀   ❀   ❀   ❀   ❀

Let's Have More Fun! The birthday boy or girl gets an early start for the party by brush painting or finger painting the invitations on plain pieces of white paper. After they dry, fold the paper into halves or fourths and print the appropriate party information with a felt tip pen.

For edible decorations, make different colors of Jell-O and put each color into individual clear glass bowls. Place the bowls on cardboard cut out in the shape of a palette.

Draw pictures of paintbrushes in bright colors and hang them around the house for festive decorations.

Encourage the kids to use their own imaginations to create their masterpieces. However, if they are getting stuck or frustrated you might try these ideas. Give them an abstract word to illustrate such as *love* or *family*. Or have them listen to music and paint their reactions to it. You can also try showing them Impressionist paintings or modern paintings and have them try to copy the style.

In addition to painting pictures, the older children could also paint T-shirts with fabric markers, or ceramic figures with tempera paints. Besides using watercolors, younger children can finger paint while older children use acrylic or oil paints.

Another fun activity is cutting out cookies from prepared cookie dough and painting them with egg yolk–based paints made by adding food coloring to egg yolks.

❀ Doll's Tea Party ❀

Lesley Fuller
Grand Ledge, Michigan

Age Group: Three to six years old
Invitations: Lace paper doilies
Special Theme Food: Tea sandwiches, pretend "tea"
Decorations: Lace doilies, small paper parasols, dolls in fancy dress-up clothes
Activities: Teacup relay race, stop-the-music teacup game
Goodie Bag: Toys and clothing for dolls

❀   ❀   ❀   ❀   ❀

Here's What to Do: How about a Doll's Tea Party for little girls from three to six years old? We did it, and it was a lot of fun for everyone, both parents and children.

Every girl who comes to the birthday party brings her favorite dolly all dressed up in her fanciest clothes. A small table is set up with chairs and places for both the children and their dolls.

We served "tea," which was really juice in children's teacups, and fancy grown-up tea sandwiches with the crusts cut off for the guests. Pretend tea and sandwiches—empty teacups and play food—were served to the dolls. Of course, the little girls fed their dolls as well as themselves.

The party favors were doll items, including clothes, comb and brush sets, doll house furniture, little baby bottles, and other inexpensive things to go along with them.

❀   ❀   ❀   ❀   ❀

Let's Have More Fun! Write the invitations on lace paper doilies.

For decorations, hang up lace paper doilies of different sizes and shapes, put small paper parasols on the table, and seat dressed-up dolls in small chairs.

Set out place cards around the table for both the "mommies" and their "babies." Write in the names of the dolls as the guests arrive.

Have relay races, with the children going back and forth across the room balancing a plastic teacup and saucer on their heads.

Sit the children in a circle and have them pass around a small teacup filled with beans or marbles while music plays. If any of the beans or marbles spill out of the cup, the person doing the spilling must hold on to the cup until the spilled beans or marbles are returned

They're a Must

Several large plastic garbage bags are a must for any birthday party. They can be used for easy cleanups of the table after everyone has eaten the cake, ice cream, and other gooey stuff.

In addition, as each present is opened, immediately throw away the wrapping paper from that gift. Discarding the paper right away will keep the party room neat, help prevent gifts from getting misplaced, and, most importantly, avoid the trauma of having a new toy accidentally thrown away along with a large pile of gift wrapping paper that has accumulated on the floor.

to the cup. The person holding the cup when the music stops is out. The last person left in the game wins.

❀ Football Tailgate Party ❀

Amanda Philpot
Newport, Ohio

Age Group: Eight to twelve years old
Invitations: Small footballs or football-shaped invitations
Special Theme Food: Tailgate party foods, football-shaped cake
Decorations: Pom-poms and team pennants
Activities: Frisbee, touch football, watching football game on television
Goodie Bag: Pom-poms, team pennants, small footballs

❀   ❀   ❀   ❀   ❀

Here's What to Do: Football is really a big thing here in the Columbus area because of Ohio State University, so we had a football tailgate party for our son's eighth birthday. It helps if you have a station wagon, but you can still do a tailgate party even if you don't. Just set up a couple of card tables in your driveway or on your lawn.

If you think you need a station wagon to have a tailgate party just go to any football stadium before a game and see all the different setups people have, not to mention the lavish food spreads and decorations. At our son's tailgate party we had all the things we have seen at football games: a small hibachi-type grill, a cooler filled with soda, hamburgers, hot dogs, sausages, grilled shrimp, potato salad, chips, plastic plates and silverware, plastic cups, and lots of napkins. You get the idea.

If the parents of your son's friends are into football they could be invited, too, and it makes for a nice afternoon. We asked our son's friends and their parents to wear football sweatshirts, jerseys, or baseball hats, all emblazoned with their favorite teams' logos. Around here, naturally, it was Ohio State. We had several footballs to throw around and a boom box for music.

Of course, the birthday cake was in the shape of a football. One of our friends who hosted a really elaborate reunion party had a cake made in the shape of a stadium complete with goal posts, but that could be a little too expensive.

There is one consideration, though. You do need nice weather to have the Tailgate Party. The best time of the year is the fall, of course, since everyone is excited about football, but the weather can be iffy depending on where you live. Have a plan to move the party indoors in case of rain or an early snow.

If you do have to move inside, you can turn on the television if there's a football game scheduled. You can still cook outside and bring the food indoors. If you plan this party around a big football game, the kids might want to watch the game anyway!

❀   ❀   ❀   ❀   ❀

Let's Have More Fun! For invitations that can be hand delivered, get small, inexpensive footballs and write the party information right on the balls. For the invitations that must be mailed, cut out football-shaped pieces of light brown cardboard, draw the laces and the seams, and write the necessary information in pen.

Place a few pom-poms and team pennants around on the lawn for stadium atmosphere decorations.

For take-home goodies, give the guests footballs, team pennants, and pom-poms in their team's colors.

❀ Farm Party ❀

Saul Kuehn
Richfield, Minnesota

Age Group: Four to six years old
Invitations: Pictures of farm animals
Special Theme Food: Hearty farm fare, farmyard cake
Decorations: Toy animals, pictures of farms and farm animals
Activities: Playing with farm toys, animal-themed contests
Goodie Bag: Bandanna, farm animals, and basket

❀   ❀   ❀   ❀   ❀

Here's What to Do: Every kid likes the idea of living on a farm, since they have no idea of all the work they would have to do if they actually lived on one. I know . . . I grew up on one. I don't miss all the work, but I sure liked the idea of farms and farming, so we had a Farm Party for our daughter's sixth birthday.

There are a lot of farms in Minnesota but few of the boys and girls who came to the party really knew what a farm was like, so we didn't have to be too accurate. My wife grew up in an apartment building in Chicago, so anything I said about a farm she believed. (On the other hand, she tells me stories about growing up in the big city, and I have no way of knowing if she's telling me the truth.)

For the party, each child who comes gets a small plastic farm animal. They get their choice from a "barnyard" setup that you can see as soon as you come into the house. Then a name tag with the child's name is attached to the chosen animal.

Set up a toy farm on the floor with a barn, fences, feeding places, tractors, and other farm things for the children to play with, including their own animal.

Hold a contest to see who can make the sound most like his animal; who can walk the most like his animal; and for real fun, although a little messy, who can eat the most like his animal. The parents should try and close their eyes for this last contest. Have first, second, and third prizes for each contest so every guest gets to win at least one prize.

The cake should be a flat sheet cake decorated like a farm with plastic fences, a silo, a farmhouse, a barn, a tractor, and other things usually seen around a farm. A hobby store will probably have the farm buildings and equipment, since they sell them for model train layouts.

Napkins should be red-and-white checkered bandannas, and the food should be hearty farm fare, not fancy stuff. Serve hard-boiled eggs, hamburgers, fried chicken, potatoes, pickles, rolls, and chocolate bars.

Each child takes home a bandanna and farm animal in a little basket with a tag saying "The———Farm," using your last name to personalize it.

❀   ❀   ❀   ❀   ❀

Let's Have More Fun! Make the invitations by cutting out color pictures of farm animals and farm and rural scenes from magazines. Paste them onto green construction paper and write the necessary information in pen around the picture.

Besides hobby shops, you can try a five-and-ten or one of those "dollar" stores for the toy farm animals and equipment. Place toy farm animals on the table and on various pieces of furniture. Hang up pictures of farmers and farm scenes for the right setting. Then, in addition to the farm animal they received upon arrival, guests get to fill up their goodie bag basket with the animals used as decorations.

❀ Beachless Beach Party ❀

Agnes Thaxton
Dunbar, West Virginia

Age Group: Four to eight years old
Invitations: Invitations shaped like sunglasses
Special Theme Food: Boardwalk seashore foods, "sand pail" cake
Decorations: Painted seashore backdrop, seashells, assorted beach items
Activities: Picture taking, beach picnic, beach games
Goodie Bag: Pail and shovel

❀ ❀ ❀ ❀ ❀

Here's What to Do: I really like this idea for a birthday party if the party is in the middle of winter or if you live far from the ocean or a lake with a beach. Think of it as a beach party without all the sand and mess.

If you are having the party in the winter ask the guests to wear bathing suits and turn the heat up to about eighty degrees. Play music by the Beach Boys or have summertime party music. Although it might be a little greasy, you can spread a tiny amount of sunscreen on each child. Be sure to check with their parents first to get permission to do this, since some children may have sensitive skin.

An added feature, if you are good with art or have a talented friend, is to paint a beach and ocean backdrop and take Polaroid pictures of people in their bathing suits in front of the painted backdrop.

The foods selected for the party are boardwalk-resort–type foods like cotton candy (you can get a machine from a party rental store), hot dogs, hamburgers, ice-cream cones, snow cones, caramel popcorn, saltwater taffy, fudge, and other foods you remember from your trips to the shore. Candy, cookies, and other foods can be served informally on paper plates. Beach buckets and shovels are taken home as party favors.

There is one note of caution. As much as you might want to make this an authentic beach party, don't, *absolutely do not*, place buckets of real sand in your living room or use sand in any way for the party. It will spread all over your house and you will never, ever, get it all cleaned up. I know, because it happened to me.

❀   ❀   ❀   ❀   ❀

Let's Have More Fun! Make the invitations in the shape of sunglasses, cut out from thin cardboard. Decorate the front of the glasses with glitter, colorful designs, or stickers. Put the time, date, and other information about the party on the back side of the glasses.

To help set the mood, instead of sitting at a table, spread beach towels around on the floor for the children to sit on when they eat. You can also scatter seashells, beach balls, soft Frisbees, and inflatable toys around the party room.

In keeping with the theme of the party, have a "pail and shovel" birthday cake. Just make a regular white cake and cut it into pieces so it fits into a clean or new beach pail. Put white frosting between the layers and top with crushed vanilla wafers that will look like sand. Place candies shaped like fish and seashells in the crushed cookie "sand."

The kids can toss fish-shaped bean bags into pails, with prizes awarded for accuracy, fish with toy fishing rods for toys in a water-filled tub, and play quiet board games like checkers and Snakes and Ladders.

You can play volleyball with a blown-up beach ball if you clear a large enough area.

❀ A Man's Party ❀

Martie Schroeder
Albuquerque, New Mexico

Age Group: Ten to twelve years old
Invitations: Regular adult party invitations
Special Theme Food: Adult barbecue, cake
Decorations: None
Activities: Adult backyard games
Goodie Bag: "Mature" toys

❀   ❀   ❀   ❀   ❀

Here's What to Do: There's nothing that young boys like better than being treated as if they are grown up, so consider giving a "grown-up" adult barbecue party for your son.

There are no decorations or little kid birthday trappings like hats or noisemakers. All his friends—just boys or it could include some girls if he likes that idea—are invited over for a backyard barbecue dinner (not lunch, since this is an adult event).

Have hot dogs, hamburgers, baked potatoes, grilled vegetables, garden salad, corn on the cob, and other adult foods. If your budget permits, you could even have steak, pork chops, or fish on the grill. Another possibility is to have skewers with shish kebabs of onions, peppers, and meat.

Set up an outdoor table with serious plastic plates and utensils, not birthday plates, and have a cooler with ice and cans of soda where the guests can serve themselves.

You can have guests help with the grilling but with very close adult supervision. Take orders from all the guests for what they want and cook each one's food to order, adding to the adult way of doing things.

The condiments, in addition to the usual ketchup and mustard, could also include chutney, corn relish, honey mustard, and other grown-up tastes.

For games, play Frisbee, touch football, horseshoes, and other adult backyard activities.

The birthday cake shouldn't be too childish, perhaps a sophisticated hazelnut or "rum" cake from a good bakery with just a couple of candles on it. When it's time to blow out the candles, keep it low-keyed, but remember that it is a nice tradition that even grown-ups enjoy.

Although adults might not open their gifts during a party, you could make an exception in this case and have the birthday boy—oops, birthday man—open them so his friends can enjoy seeing all the presents.

Exchanging Information

The night before the party you might want to call all the parents of the guests to get an exact—or as exact as possible—count of how many children you can expect to be there.

Your telephone call will also be a reminder to anyone who has forgotten about the party or who is not sure of the time and date. And your call can provide answers to any questions people have. You'll want to remind them, as well, about when the party ends.

—Tess Wheeler
Newton, Iowa

❀   ❀   ❀   ❀   ❀

Let's Have More Fun! Use regular store-bought invitations that would be used for an adult party.

Although party favors are not necessary for such "big kids" at this party, toys like a Frisbee or a chess/checkers set would be appropriate.

❀ Make-It and Bake-It Party ❀

Jill Vaccaro
Hollywood, Florida

Age Group: Four to twelve years old
Invitations: Chef's hat invitations
Special Theme Food: Cold cuts sandwiches and cake or ice-cream sundaes
Decorations: Pictures depicting food and food-related items
Activities: Making lunch and dessert
Goodie Bag: Personalized aprons or chef's hats or parfait glasses

❀   ❀   ❀   ❀   ❀

Here's What to Do: Years ago, a kitchen do-it-yourself lunch and baking party would be for girls only, but with more and more boys involved in cooking, you could do this type of party for both boys and girls.

The party should be held at noontime, since people will be eating lunch as part of the party.

Set out on a kitchen counter cold cuts, cheese, tuna salad, egg salad, sliced eggs, washed and dried lettuce leaves, tomatoes, and whatever other sandwich makings you desire. Have several types of bread available as well as mayonnaise, mustard, ketchup, and other spreads. Use paper plates, plastic utensils, paper cups, and other disposable items. Beverages could include sodas, juices, and chocolate milk. Everyone gets to make his own sandwiches and takes a place at the table.

After everyone is finished eating lunch and the place is cleaned up, it's time to bake the birthday cake, birthday cupcakes, or birthday brownies. Have several boxes of mixes along with all the ingredients that have to be added and make sure you have the right baking pans ready.

Everyone gets to help make the dessert, and afterward can add an assortment of decorations such as nuts, sprinkles, and small candies. Make sure to have lots of frosting, too!

❀   ❀   ❀   ❀   ❀

Let's Have More Fun! Make invitations from white paper cut out in the shape of chef's hats. Stick a fancy toothpick through the bottom of the hat for decoration.

Create a delicatessen atmosphere with pictures of sandwiches, pickles, fountain drinks, and so on. Put fancy toothpicks in the cold cuts and have fancy paper napkins on the table.

While the desserts are baking, occupy the children by making cleanup time a fun time. Assign jobs to everyone, and have them help out by setting up the frosting and other dessert decorations.

If there is not enough time for baking dessert or if you do not want to have the younger children working around a hot oven, make ice-cream sundaes instead. Put out cartons of several different flavors of ice cream along with different toppings like flavored syrups, a variety of small candies, cans of whipped cream, and jams.

Each guest gets an apron or chef's hat with his or her name on it to wear while making sandwiches and dessert and to take home.

If you decide to make ice-cream sundaes, get colorful plastic parfait glasses that the children can make their sundaes in. After the glasses are washed out they can be taken home as a party favor. For a baking party, you can also give aprons, small cookbooks, or a set of recipe cards as take-home favors.

Oops!

When you have a houseful of excited children enjoying a party you never know what kinds of spills or bumps might happen regardless of how careful or optimistic you might be, so, as the Boy Scouts say, "Be prepared."

Keep within easy reach a roll of paper towels, some cleaning solution, a bottle of club soda, and anything else you usually use for those minor household accidents.

Now you will not get so upset when the inevitable soda spills or the chocolate icing gets on the rug, since you will be ready when it happens.

❀ Mystery Party ❀

Ina Kerr
Newark, Delaware

Age Group: Five to eight years old
Invitations: Mirror-image invitations
Special Theme Food: Coded message cake
Decorations: Color-coded footprints
Activities: Following trails to mystery boxes, mystery puzzle, mystery story, mystery treasure
Goodie Bag: Detective tools

❀ ❀ ❀ ❀ ❀

Here's What to Do: It's no mystery that children love to be part of a mystery. So why not give them one for their party?

When the children first come through the door they see yellow cutout footprints leading from the doorway through the house to a large closed yellow carton. When the children open the box each one finds a yellow bag, sealed shut, with his or her name on it, and removes it from the box. Then they follow blue footprints to another large box, this one blue, and take out their blue bags, also with their name on it and sealed shut. Next, red footprints lead to a red box with similar bags inside. Depending on the size and layout of your home, the trails of different colored footprints will intersect and cross over at some points.

Now, what is in the bags? Lunch!

Divide the following items among the bags: a sandwich, plastic spoons and forks, napkins, small party favors, wrapped candies and cookies, and chilled juice boxes.

You could also include one puzzle piece in each bag. When the pieces from all the bags are joined, a mystery picture is revealed. Another fun thing is including a series of beginning mystery story lines, one in each bag, that the children must add to, making up a mystery story. There could also be clues to a hidden mystery treasure that must be solved, with prizes for everyone.

The birthday cake should be a mystery, too, with a coded message on top that can be decoded with a code key hidden somewhere in the party room. The code could be a simple Z=A, Y=B, X=C or 1=A, 2=B, 3=C, or complicated, depending on the age of the children.

Try These Mystery Openers

"It was a dark and stormy night . . ."
"The body fell with a thud . . ."
"The first thing I heard was a loud scream . . ."
" 'Help!' she yelled . . ."

❀   ❀   ❀   ❀   ❀

Let's Have More Fun! Write the invitations backward so they must be held up to a mirror in order to be read.

A good take-home goodie bag could include a magnifying glass, a small note pad, a pen or pencil, and a detective badge.

A Personal Touch

All the goodie bags do not have to contain the same things for everyone. Since there probably will be children of different ages at your party, it's a good idea if there are different things in the goodie bags you give to each guest to take home. Think of the age of each guest and fill his or her bag with the appropriate items.

You can even take this idea a step further. If you are well acquainted with the children coming to the party, each bag could be customized for the person getting it. It is a little more work, but the time and effort are worth it.

If you do this, don't forget to mark each bag with the name of the child it's meant for!

—Terrie Sandoval
White Rock, New Mexico

❀ Dog Party ❀

Edna Dabney
Petersburg, Virginia

Age Group: Three to five years old
Invitations: Real dog biscuits wrapped with paper
Special Theme Food: Food eaten from dog food dishes, dog-shaped cake
Decorations: Pictures of dogs
Activities: Veterinarian clinic, Musical Bone game, Matching Tails and Ears game, dog show
Goodie Bag: Toy dogs and dog food dishes

❀   ❀   ❀   ❀   ❀

Here's What to Do: Our family is a big dog family—we have four of them—so we had a Dog Party for our daughter when she turned seven years old. A Dog Party doesn't need real dogs, although our four dogs did attend.

Each person who came to the party got a stuffed toy dog, personalized by a tag with her name on it. The tags had a place to write the name chosen for the stuffed dog. Of course, they all got to take home the dog.

We served hot dogs in dog food dishes and the birthday cake was shaped like a dog biscuit. The cake could also look like a bone, a doghouse, or a dog.

For one game, pretend that each dog has a malady and set up a veterinarian clinic. You and several of the children could play the role of the vet.

Another game to play is Musical Bone, which is like musical chairs. Play music as the children pass around a toy dog bone and whoever has the bone when the music stops is out. The last player remaining is the winner.

Then there is the Matching Tails and Ears game. Cut out pictures of dogs and then cut off the ears and tails. The children try to match the tails and ears with the pictures of the dogs.

There could also be a show with the children exhibiting their toy dogs. Every dog would get a prize ribbon for something special like best coat, brightest eyes, longest tail, and so on.

❀   ❀   ❀   ❀   ❀

Let's Have More Fun! Write the invitations on plain white paper, cut to size, and wrap each invitation around a dog biscuit. You can also buy bone-shaped cookie cutters and make cookie "dog biscuits," and wrap the invitations around them. The cookies would also be fun treats at the party.

For the decorations, hang up pictures of all kinds of dogs and scatter around real dog biscuits.

Along with the toy dogs, guests take home their dog food dishes after they are washed out.

❀ Tall Tales Party ❀

Kitty Barnhouse Purgason
Pasadena, California

Age Group: Five to ten years old
Invitations: Picture of Paul Bunyan and his ox, Babe
Special Theme Food: Pancakes, popcorn, sausages, pancake birthday cake
Decorations: None
Activities: Storytelling, bear toss, hammering game
Goodie Bag: Rope rattlesnakes, water pistols

❀   ❀   ❀   ❀   ❀

Here's What to Do: When our son was nearing five years old, his favorite read-aloud stories were the tall tales of heroes like Paul Bunyan and Pecos Bill. So for his fifth birthday we had a Tall Tales Party.

The party in our backyard was organized around storytelling and activities reflecting the kind of things the heroes did in the tall tales. Although I used picture books, the stories were told in my own words to keep the pace in line with the attention span of a dozen excited young boys. (The fantastically illustrated books by Steven Kellogg are especially good.)

We began with the story of Mike Fink, the crack shot, wrestler of bears, and king of the keelboatmen on the Mississippi River. After this story the boys drew their own targets on big pieces of newsprint and were given water pistols to try to hit the bull's-eye. The water pistols went home with them as favors.

Next they tried to wrestle a bear and throw him all the way to the Rocky Mountains. A map of the United States was drawn in chalk on our driveway and the boys threw a giant stuffed bear as far as they could.

Then it was time for Pecos Bill, who turned a rattlesnake into the first lariat and herded the longhorn steers of Texas. Each boy got a length of rope and was helped to glue on a red pipe cleaner for the tongue, green wiggly eyes, and a rattle to make it a rattlesnake. The rattles were inch-long lengths of plastic straws with a few grains of rice inside and taped at both ends. The "snakes" were tied into lassos, and all the boys got a chance to rope a steer: a longhorn head cut out from heavy cardboard and nailed to an old chair. The rattlesnakes were taken home as party favors.

The next story was John Henry, the legendary hammerman who won a contest with a steam drill. (Julius Lester and Jerry Pinkney have a wonderfully illustrated version of this story.)

The activity for John Henry was hammering, of course, and was a big hit with five-year-old boys. We got chunks of soft, easy-to-break rocks and rubber mallets and everyone got a chance to pound rocks like John Henry. Safety goggles were used during the rock hammering.

Finally, we read the story of Paul Bunyan, logger. No, we did not have the boys chopping down trees, although they would have loved to. Instead, we focused on the appetite of Paul and his ox team for flapjacks.

We prepared a bunch of pancakes in advance and got two big frying pans—the ones we use for camping. The boys were divided into two teams and had a contest to see who could flip pancakes the most without having them fly out of the pan.

The birthday lunch consisted of popcorn, sausages, and, of course, pancakes. To make the pancakes as special as a birthday cake, we added whipped cream and strawberries. The birthday boy got a big stack of them with candles.

For the boys who arrived early, got picked up late, or didn't feel like participating in an activity, we had some pages photocopied from one of the tall tales books that they could color.

"This is the best party I've been to!" we heard again and again.

If you have girls, you might want to add the stories of some female tall tale heroines. Two great illustrated children's books for the girls are *Swamp Angel* and *Sally Thunder Ann Crockett*.

❀　　　❀　　　❀　　　❀　　　❀

Let's Have More Fun! For invitations, photocopy pictures of Paul Bunyan and his blue ox, Babe, or any other character from a tall tale that will be read at the party. Write all the party information on the photocopied picture.

❀ Off-Season Snow Party ❀

Gloria Landry
Worcester, Massachusetts

Age Group: Seven to nine years old
Invitations: White confetti in envelopes
Special Theme Food: White foods, "ski slope" cake
Decorations: White streamers, snowflakes
Activities: Pin the Hat on the Snowman, making paper and Styrofoam snowmen
Goodie Bag: Paper and Styrofoam snowmen

❀   ❀   ❀   ❀   ❀

Here's What to Do: Have you ever heard of a snow birthday party in July? Although everyone thinks of snow only in the winter, an Off-Season Snow Party can be special fun in the summer when it's really hot out. And it's a special treat in places like Florida and Southern California where children rarely see snow. We had one for our nine-year-old, and she and her friends really loved it and had a fabulous time.

To start, cut out snowflakes from squares of white paper. You've probably done this with your kids: fold the paper in eighths on the diagonal, cut out fancy shapes, then unfold. Tape or glue these on long white crepe paper streamers, and hang these from the ceiling. Make more paper snowflakes and spread them around the room, on the table, and on the floor. Have a white tablecloth with white plates, cups, and napkins.

For the birthday treat you should make a white cake, covered with white icing and sprinkled with flaked coconut. Cut and stack pieces of the cake so it resembles a ski slope. Buy small people figures and place them as if they are skiing down the slope. Colored toothpicks can be placed along the slope as ski trail markers. Serve thick slices of the cake with vanilla ice cream or whipped cream.

For the main meal have white bread sandwiches with white cheese with vanilla milk shakes.

Play Pin the Hat on the Snowman. Draw a large snowman and hang it on the wall. Draw and cut out many small hats and use them as the game pieces the children try to pin on the snowman.

The children can cut out snowmen and accessories such as mittens, scarves, and gloves from construction paper and paste the snowmen together. Then they color the snowmen. The snowmen are taken home as a party favor.

Let's Have More Fun! Sprinkling white confetti inside the invitations will start to put people in the mood for going to a Snow Party.

Make snowmen out of different-size Styrofoam balls stuck together with toothpicks. Create the accessories such as hats, buttons, scarves, and gloves from pipe cleaners and small fabric scraps.

A snowball fight with cotton ball "snowballs" is great fun. No one will get hurt—and nothing will get broken.

For take-home favors you can also include real scarves or mittens.

Write It Down

Have a pen and pad right there when the presents are opened so you can write down who has given what.

No matter how good your memory, it is really difficult, if not impossible with all the distractions and excitement of an ongoing party, to match guests with their presents without a written record.

You will be happy you have a list of who gave which present when it is time to write thank-you notes.

❀ Airplane Party ❀

Bernadette Schmidt
Pleasantville, New Jersey

Age Group: Six to nine years old
Invitations: Wooden glider kit with information written on the airplane parts
Special Theme Food: Your choice, served on trays
Decorations: Pictures of airplanes and clouds
Activities: Making paper airplanes, visiting an airport
Goodie Bag: Toy airplanes in "baggage"

❀   ❀   ❀   ❀   ❀

Here's What to Do: The kids will really like an airplane party. Hang pictures of clouds and airplanes around the room for decoration.

Use a map or several maps taped together for a tablecloth. Serve the meal on small trays—plastic ones bought at a party store, cardboard ones you make yourself, or small disposable tin trays. Put the food on the trays and cover tightly with plastic wrap so they look like the meals served on airplanes. The food should be simple, maybe cut-up hot dogs or chicken and a vegetable like carrots and peas, or whatever else your child likes. It just has to fit neatly in the tray compartments. Also put the plastic silverware and a napkin in plastic wrap. Use a wagon or a tea cart to serve the drinks around the room so it's like the beverage cart.

If you live near an airport, plan ahead to see if the children can go look at the planes or take a tour.

Before everyone leaves the party, they go to a "baggage claim" area in the house identified with a big sign. There they pick up their suitcases, which have a toy airplane inside. You could make suitcases from shoe boxes by painting them and attaching a heavy ribbon on top for the handle. Make claim checks to give to each person that matches a tag on a shoe box suitcase.

❀   ❀   ❀   ❀   ❀

Let's Have More Fun! Get balsa wood glider kits and write all the party information on the wings or on the fuselage. Send the airplane invitations unassembled.

Show the children how to make simple paper airplanes and go outside to fly them.

Have a variety of colored papers of different sizes for making them. If desired, get a book on more elaborate paper airplanes and have adults make these advanced models for the children to play with.

Have plastic or metal airplanes for the take-home toys along with the paper airplanes made during the party.

When Timing Is Important

When sending out the party invitations be sure to indicate both the starting time and the ending time of the party. If you don't put the time the party will be over, some parents might not show up until long after the party has ended.

While a two-hour birthday party might seem reasonable to you and you expect everyone to be gone after two hours and fifteen minutes, someone will surely think the party will last for three or four hours and not show up when required unless definitely told when to do so.

—Olga Fowler
Aurora, Illinois

❀ Dump Truck Party ❀

Julius Dwyer
Shorewood, Wisconsin

Age Group: Four to eight years old
Invitations: Truck Wheel
Special Theme Food: Food served in trucks
Decorations: Pictures of road signs and toy road signs
Activities: Pin the Wheel on the Truck game
Goodie Bag: Toy trucks, car keys, and computer-generated driver's license

❀   ❀   ❀   ❀   ❀

Here's What to Do: So much effort is put into parties for girls that sometimes I think my son loses out. Most little boy parties are just food and playing ball. Many parents don't give enough thought to their boys' parties because they're just boys and boys don't care.

But boys do care.

When my son wanted a special party for his seventh birthday I decided that it would be more than just candy, cake, soda, and running around the house making noise.

So we had a Dump Truck Party!

We bought a plastic dump truck about a foot long for every boy attending. It is not too expensive if you look around different stores for suitable trucks and then ask for a little discount if you are buying ten or fifteen trucks. Try to get trucks of different colors. The trucks do not have to be exactly alike as long as they are all dump trucks.

Set up the trucks so you can serve the food in the back of each one for each boy who's there. Put the cake, candy, ice cream, and whatever you're having right in the truck.

Put a bigger truck in the center of the table with cupcakes, candy bars, or other solid foods stacked like cargo on the truck and let the birthday boy roll the truck around delivering the goods to everyone there. Another truck could have chocolate chips in it.

One of the games the boys played is Pin the Wheel on the Truck taken from the old Pin the Tail on the Donkey game. Cut out a picture of a truck—or draw one yourself—and each boy gets a picture of a wheel to pin onto the truck where the wheels go.

If you have a computer or someone who can do graphics for you, make driver's licenses to give to the boys as they leave. All the boys also take home the dump truck they had at the table.

❀   ❀   ❀   ❀   ❀

When Two Is Better Than One

If you have a large extended family or a large group of adult friends who must be invited to your child's birthday party, consider having two separate parties: one for the adults and one just for the children.

When you have one party for everyone and it's a large group, the birthday boy or girl can get lost in the festivities, since so much attention is placed on keeping the adults entertained and happy.

With two parties you will serve your child better on that special day.

—Celeste Eubanks
Jacksonville, Arkansas

Let's Have More Fun! For invitations, make a wheel design on thin cardboard, cut it out, and write party information in travel terms: Driver (name of birthday boy); Destination (address of party); Estimated Time of Arrival (date and time of the party).

Hang up pictures of road signs and place toy road signs around the table.

Put old car keys on a key chain that has a truck logo and give out as party favors.

✿ Half-Birthday Party ✿

Denise M. Napiwocki
La Crescenta, California

Age Group: Five to ten years old
Invitations: Two-color paper
Special Theme Food: Foods served in halves
Decorations: Pictures of half-moons, half sandwiches, half cakes, half balloons
Activities: Half versions of games
Goodie Bag: Checkers

✿   ✿   ✿   ✿   ✿

Here's What to Do: Consider celebrating a child's birthday at the six-month mark if the actual birthday falls too close to the holidays or is in the middle of summer when their special friends are away. We have celebrated several half-birthdays—a really fun and creative idea—in our family.

    When our son was six and a half years old we had a half-birthday party in the park.

72

We invited children from age five to seven, who thoroughly enjoyed learning about one-half in such a fun way.

Send out invitations on paper that is half one color, half another. You will also want to start the party at half-past the hour.

Cut place mats out of cardboard and have the guests decorate each half differently. Buy two different kinds of party hats, cut them in half, and then tape two different halves together.

Party activities are around the theme of one-half. Hold relay races with half running, half skipping. Cut balls in half and toss at half a target.

The refreshments follow the same theme, with a half-birthday cake or a whole one decorated one-half one way, the other half another. Put out a bowl of chips, half potato and half corn.

Checkers are an ideal party favor, of course, as they are half red and half black.

End the party in one-and-a-half or two-and-a-half hours.

A half-party has endless possibilities, it just takes a little imagination: half yours, half your child's.

Try it, it isn't half bad.

> ### Two . . . to Be Sure
>
> Since what can go wrong will be sure to happen when you are getting ready for the party, have a second birthday outfit ready and available for the guest of honor in case of last-minute spills, rips, falling down into mud, and other fashion disasters.

❋　　❋　　❋　　❋　　❋

Let's Have More Fun! Buy party decorations and cut them in half. Hang the halves around the room.

Fix the birthday boy's or girl's clothes so they are dressed half one color and half another. They'll look just right for a half-birthday party. Wear mis-matched socks and shoes from two separate pairs.

❀ Splash Party ❀

Ivy Hardy
Rockville, Maryland

Age Group: One to six years old
Invitations: Small inflatable toys with party information written on them
Special Theme Food: Simple take-along foods and fish-shaped candies
Decorations: Beach toys
Activities: Water games
Goodie Bag: Water toys

❀   ❀   ❀   ❀   ❀

Here's What to Do: A summer splash party is perfect for youngsters. It gives them a chance to play on their own without having to be amused every minute. But, of course, close parental supervision is necessary.

Set up several kiddie pools in your backyard. Be prepared to replace the water several times as the water gets splashed out, crumbs and other food parts get in the water, and in case one of the guests has an accident during the party. For older children, sprinklers are fun, and if you can set up several, you can hold races or play Follow the Leader through them.

Have enough water toys, including water pistols, plastic fish, boats, and small inflatable toys, so all the children have a choice of what they want to play with.

Make sure the parents know that it is going to be a pool party so the children will arrive in bathing suits. A clean, dry outfit for after the party is over is convenient for children who have a long distance to travel home. Have a good supply of towels for everyone to dry off.

The entire party is kept outdoors, so the food will be relatively simple: for example, peanut butter and jelly sandwiches, juice in plastic pitchers or in juice boxes, individual bags of potato chips, and M&M's candies.

In keeping with the idea of serving easy foods outside, cupcakes are better than a big birthday cake so you don't need plates and forks for serving. Be sure to decorate the cupcakes brightly, with frosting and sprinkles. Put out fish-shaped candies in different colors. Of course, the birthday boy's or girl's cupcake should have candles on it.

❀   ❀   ❀   ❀   ❀

Help Is Nearby

Here is one way to make your party a lot easier so you can enjoy it more yourself rather than running around in a frenzy doing everything without any help.

Hire a teenager—a reliable and good baby-sitter type—as a helper to be another pair of hands and feet at the party. She or he can help serve the food, clean up, take care of the guests, and be a real party-giving assistant for a very modest cost.

—Christine Coyle
Johnston, Rhode Island

Let's Have More Fun! For the invitations, get small inflatable toys. Write all the information about the party on the toys. If necessary, blow up the toys before writing on them. Let the invitations dry before deflating and mailing.

As favors, the guests get to take home the water toys they were playing with during the party.

❀ Carnival Party ❀

Kim Newsholme
Royal Palm Beach, Florida

Age Group: Six to twelve years old
Invitations: Sent with carnival tickets
Special Theme Food: Carnival food
Decorations: Carnival midway
Activities: Carnival games
Goodie Bag: Small toy game prizes

❀　　　❀　　　❀　　　❀　　　❀

Here's What to Do: For my son's seventh birthday party we had a carnival.

Get four heavy cardboard boxes from an appliance store and a roll of tickets from a party supply store. Cut the boxes so they look like carnival booths and spray paint them with wild colors or funny faces. Each box will be used for a different game.

When the guests arrive, hand out generous numbers of tickets to each person, the same number to everyone. Use the tickets as "admission" to play games and "buy" food.

At our party the kids had to pay for everything with their tickets—they were in control of the fun and the food.

For the first game booth (a decorated carton), set up a game of Knock-down the Cans. Set six cans in a pyramid and have beanbags for the kids to toss. For the second booth, try Pop the Balloons. Pin or tape blown-up balloons to thick cardboard, and have darts for the kids to toss. This booth will need extra adult supervision. Also, remember the more the balloons are inflated, the easier to pop them. Now in booth number three we had a game that could be called Trick or Treat? or "Surprise or Be Surprised." We cut three small round doors in number three and someone was in the box. When the kids opened a door, they either got a toy (a small truck or doll) or they were surprised with a pie in the face. The kids went wild. Have prizes for all of the booths.

Booth number four was the food place. We stapled bags of cotton candy onto that box. There was a sign posted that said "cotton candy—3 coupons," "hot dogs—4 coupons," "soda—2 coupons," and "ice cones—2 coupons."

This party was so much fun that my son and his friends have requested it again.

❀   ❀   ❀   ❀   ❀

Be Prepared

You might not think it is necessary to include this reminder in a party book, but too often I have heard about forgotten cameras, not enough film, or a video camera with a dead battery. Make sure you have enough film, fresh batteries in your camera, and that the camera is handy before the party starts.

—Sabrina Conley
Grand Prairie, Texas

Let's Have More Fun! Include several tickets with each invitation to get people starting to think about going to carnival.

A cake baked with hidden surprises—M&M's, peppermints, chocolate chips, and other candies—will add to the carnival atmosphere.

❀ Color Party ❀

Ada Jarrett
Lawrence, Indiana

Age Group: Three to six years old
Invitations: Color coded for each guest
Special Theme Food: Different colored cupcakes
Decorations: Color-coordinated place settings, solid color pictures
Activities: Scavenger hunt, naming game, painting
Goodie Bag: Painting equipment, color-coordinated toys

❀   ❀   ❀   ❀   ❀

Here's What to Do: Here is something my mother thought up when I was five years old, and we have used it for our children, too.

Have a Color Party. When you send out the invitations for the party, indicate on each invitation the color selected for that child. If for some reason the guest doesn't like the color you have picked out, have an alternate or two to offer. As much as possible all the children should wear outfits of their designated color.

Each person who comes has a place set at the table completely equipped—place mat, napkin, plastic spoon and fork—in his or her color. Also, at each place have a grab bag with toys, stickers, pins, and other things all in the particular color.

Organize a scavenger hunt with each person looking for items that you have hidden that are either his color or wrapped in his color of paper. Another game would be to see who could name the most things of their color. You have to be sure that you use only easy colors so every child has an equal and fair chance in this game.

As a souvenir of the birthday party, each boy or girl has a canvas or board and paints a picture in his or her color.

Follow through on the color theme and also provide a little learning by getting a set of colored transparent plastic pieces and demonstrating how making combinations of colors create new colors.

❀　　　❀　　　❀　　　❀　　　❀

Let's Have More Fun! Instead of one large birthday cake, have cupcakes, each one covered with a different color icing to match the guests.

❀ Creepy-Crawly Party ❀

Robin Landsman
Asheville, North Carolina

Age Group: Four to eight years old
Invitations: Plastic insects with invitations
Special Theme Food: Creepy-crawly cake, bug-shaped candies
Decorations: Homemade insects
Activities: Scavenger hunt, bug-themed games
Goodie Bag: Stickers and tattoos

❀   ❀   ❀   ❀   ❀

Here's What to Do: Most boys four to seven years old love creepy-crawly things, so why not have a Creepy-Crawly Birthday Party?

There are several activities for this theme.

Take plain plastic headbands and attach two pipe cleaners to resemble antennae. You can glue them on or wrap them around the headband. Glue pom-poms on the ends of the pipe cleaners. The children can then put on these insect antennae. With the antennae—

insect sensory appendages—in place, start a scavenger hunt, looking for plastic insects, spider rings, and bug-shaped candies that have already been hidden.

For the Caterpillar Crawl, divide the children up into equal groups. Then the groups stand in a straight line with their legs spread open. The last child in line crawls through the open legs of the children in front and takes his place at the front of the line. Continue the game with the "caterpillar" moving forward until all the children have crawled through to the front. The first team to have all its members crawl to the front wins.

Have a Slithering Snake relay race. In this event, children do not run but slither on their stomachs instead.

The Grasshopper Hop race has everyone hopping like a grasshopper.

For a creepy-crawly "cake," put chocolate pudding in a bowl. Stick Gummi worms into the pudding to surprise eaters and cover with a generous amount of crushed Oreo cookies to look like dirt.

Goodie bags holding bug stickers and temporary bug tattoos are given out as the guests leave for home.

❀   ❀   ❀   ❀   ❀

"Cool" Is In . . . and Essential

You can have any type of party you want for your children when they are very young because they really can't make choices for themselves and there isn't a lot of peer pressure to have the "right" kind of party.

However, once they get to be six or seven years old it is important that they get involved in all the planning so their birthday party can be exactly as they want it.

The older my boys got, the "cooler" the party had to be. Being in style and "doing the right thing" become more and more important as your children get older, and you won't know what's cool unless you ask. Trust me.

—Peggy Dager
Fort Wayne, Indiana

Let's Have More Fun! Put an assortment of plastic insects in the envelope with each invitation. It will give a creepy-crawly feeling for the party.

Get Styrofoam balls in different sizes and black pipe cleaners and use your imagination to make a variety of creepy-crawlers to place around the party room.

❀ Barney Party ❀

Selma Potter
Independence, Missouri

Age Group: Two to six years old
Invitations: Barney invitations
Special Theme Food: Food colored purple and green, apples and bananas
Decorations: Pictures of Barney, Baby Bop, and B.J.
Activities: Barney videos, "real live" Barney, taking pictures
Goodie Bag: Pictures with Barney, age-appropriate toys

❀   ❀   ❀   ❀   ❀

Here's What to Do: Little kids love that big purple dinosaur, so a Barney Party is a lot of fun. Our four-year-old son and all his guests had a marvelous time, and I am sure other children will like it, too.

If you do not have any Barney videotapes, get several from the library or tape several programs in the weeks before the party.

Cut out large cardboard outlines of Barney and color them. Make colored cutouts of Baby Bop and B.J., too.

Have Barney plates, cups, tablecloth, and napkins. The cake is in the shape of Barney and colored appropriately.

After eating, the children watch the Barney videos. If you want to take Barney to its fullest, have everyone sing "Clean Up, Clean Up," with all the children helping to clean up from the party.

Take pictures of the guests next to the large cutouts of Barney, Baby Bop, and B.J. with a Polaroid camera and give to the guests as souvenirs.

❀   ❀   ❀   ❀   ❀

Let's Have More Fun! You can buy Barney invitations already made or draw them yourself.

Use food coloring to decorate some of the food you serve. Mix together blue and red colorings to make purple.

Serve apples and bananas while singing or playing the Baby Bop song "Apples and Bananas."

Safety First

Even if you have made your home childproof for your own children, be extra cautious and make the place even more safe by removing all the things that could cause harm as well as all the things you do not want harmed. Do this well before the party, not ten minutes before the party starts.

For better or worse, your own children have a sense of what is acceptable and what is off-limits, but you certainly cannot expect your young guests attending a birthday party to know as much.

As the old saying goes, "It is better to be safe than sorry," so a close inspection of the areas where the party will be and making the necessary changes will prevent any problems later. And do not forget to check the bathroom and kitchen, special areas where there can be hazards for curious little guests not familiar with all the things you keep around the house.

Put a large bag filled with toys and decorated with pictures of Barney, Baby Bop, and B.J. on the floor and let the guests pick out toys as prizes as they leave.

A "real live" Barney can be hired to come to your party. Check the entertainment and party advertisements in your local newspapers or talk to your friends who already have had parties.

❀ High Tea Party ❀

Jennifer S. Blalock
Asheville, North Carolina

Age Group: Five to ten years old
Invitations: Invitations shaped like teacups
Special Theme Food: Foods served at an afternoon tea
Decorations: Fancy tablecloths, glitter confetti, and cutouts of fancy hand mirrors, hats, gloves, and pocketbooks
Activities: Teatime, applying makeup, and taking pictures
Goodie Bag: Beaded necklace, makeup, and photographs

❀　　　❀　　　❀　　　❀　　　❀

Here's What to Do: My daughter and I decided to have a High Tea for her eighth birthday party.

We started out with invitations shaped like teacups and saucers, and each girl's favorite doll or stuffed toy was invited, too. The guests were told to dress up for the party in something very fancy.

Next we went to the Goodwill store in town and bought my daughter a fancy prom dress at a reasonable price. Then I altered the dress so it would fit her.

The big day saw our living room decorated with construction-paper hand mirrors and other such decorations on the walls. Several card tables were set up with chairs. The tables were decorated with fancy tablecloths and heart-shaped glitter confetti was sprinkled all over.

All the girls got a big beaded necklace, also purchased at the Goodwill store, to wear as a party favor.

We served tea and punch, along with little scones, tea cakes, and dainty candies. We used real china dishes and cups so it would be fancy.

After tea, each girl was partnered with another and they were allowed to apply makeup to each other's faces. Their faces lit up when they were told they could do this, and their made-up faces were really adorable afterward. The mothers really loved this part of the party.

The makeup was bought inexpensively at a drugstore, and each girl took home some of what she used.

Pictures were taken of all the girls and their dolls, both individually and in a group, all made up and in their fancy outfits.

Save Time and Energy

Pick up the thank-you note cards at the same time you pick out the party invitations so you will have a matching set. This is especially nice if the invitations are part of the overall theme of the party. Also, keep a neat (and corrected) invitation list with all the addresses of the guests to make it easier to send out thank-you notes after the party.

Even more time can be saved if you address the thank-you notes at the same time you address the invitations.

Then my daughter opened the presents, and there was some free time for just chatting.

Everyone had such a good time that some of the guests asked their mothers if they could have a party just like this one.

❀   ❀   ❀   ❀   ❀

Let's Have More Fun! In addition to the hand mirror decorations, here are a few other things to hang up or place around the room: lace paper doilies, Victorian hand fans, and fancy hats, gloves, and pocketbooks.

❀ Cowboy Party ❀

Carrie Sherrill
Spring Valley, California

Age Group: Two to six years old
Invitations: Cowboy hat invitations
Special Theme Food: Hidden foods, cowboy hat birthday cake
Decorations: Pile of hay, piñata
Activities: Hay hunt, hayride, piñata
Goodie Bag: Bandannas, piñata toys, candy

❀   ❀   ❀   ❀   ❀

Here's What to Do: A Cowboy Party will keep energetic and fussy kids so happy and busy that they will not have any time to whine.

Start with red wagon hayrides, amusing the earlier arrivals until everyone has come.

Once everyone arrives, open a bale of hay and pile it up on the lawn. Hide packaged cookies inside and let the children have a cookie hunt.

Before the party, prepare a horse piñata and fill it with toy snakes, sheriff badges, and small boxes of raisins. Suspend this firmly at the kids' eye level and have ready blindfolds and a broom handle or other whacking tool. Let everyone take a turn and watch carefully!

Serve cake to the children outside at a small picnic table. Next, open the presents. At our party the birthday boy wore a red cowboy hat to show he was special.

❋   ❋   ❋   ❋   ❋

Let's Have More Fun! Get a bunch of brightly colored bandannas to use as napkins and to use to carry home the party favors from the piñata.

Favorite Toys

Your children probably have extra special toys that they really like more than others or especially delicate toys that must be handled very carefully.

Since there will be new guests in the home when you have the birthday party—children who may or may not be particularly careful with those special and delicate toys—it is best to put away the toys you do not want the guests playing with when they come over for the party.

If you do that, you won't spend a lot of time worrying about anything getting broken or misplaced and then having to comfort an unhappy birthday boy or girl after everyone has gone home when some toy is found broken or cannot be found at all.

❀ Show-and-tell Party ❀

Heather Simoneaux
Metairie, Louisiana

Age Group: Two to five years old
Invitations: Television with party information on screen
Special Theme Food: Favorite foods
Decorations: Streamers, balloons, other typical party decorations
Activities: Show-and-tell, sing-along
Goodie Bag: Assorted toys

❀　　　❀　　　❀　　　❀　　　❀

Here's What to Do: Since this type of party is best for preschoolers, you do not have to have a very elaborate party beyond what is described here.

You know show-and-tell from preschool, so it is easy to adopt that concept for a party.

On the invitations ask each child to bring one of her favorite things from home. The highlight of the party is show-and-tell, when the kids get to talk about what they brought.

Less Mess

A generous supply of disposable bibs ready to be used for the party guests when the ice cream and cake are served will be greatly appreciated by all the parents.

A week before the party call the parents of the guests and ask what is their child's favorite party food. Have those foods available with a sign noting whose favorite food is what. The children can also "show-and-tell" about their favorite food.

❁   ❁   ❁   ❁   ❁

Let's Have More Fun! Draw a television set and write all the party information on the screen, since this is a show-and-tell party.

Since there will be a variety of different items brought to the party for show-and-tell, it is difficult to decorate for a specific theme. Therefore, the usual brightly colored party decorations are just fine.

If the children are getting restless, why not have each child pick out a favorite song and sing it with the help of other guests?

Prepare grab bags for each guest with a variety of toys that children in their age group would enjoy. Try children's books, small candies, dolls or cars, and the perennial favorites, high-bouncing balls or colorful yo-yos.

❀ Going on a Picnic Party ❀

Alva Gundlach
Monona, Wisconsin

Age Group: Five to nine years old
Invitations: Watermelon slices and plastic ants
Special Theme Food: Picnic foods and watermelon-shaped cake
Decorations: Outdoor atmosphere
Activities: Outdoor picnic games, indoor board games
Goodie Bag: Packaged cakes, cookies, or crackers, small toys

❀   ❀   ❀   ❀   ❀

Here's What to Do: Here is a way to combine two things children really, really like—a picnic and a party. The theme for the party is Going on a Picnic.

Spread out a red-and-white checkered tablecloth or a brightly colored blanket on the floor just like a picnic blanket. Place real plants (if you have them in your house) or drawings of plants, trees, and bushes around the sides of the room to make it look like you are outdoors.

If you really want to make it look authentic, put pictures of clouds and a blue sky on the ceiling. Or you could put dark clouds on the ceiling with streamers hanging down like rain. Doesn't it always rain at picnics? Along with the rain, how about spreading around some fake ants or bugs to make it even more true to life?

Pack a big picnic basket filled with food and a picnic jug with the drinks. Use a big cooler chest with some ice containers to keep things cold. The food and drinks are up to you. Fried chicken, hard-boiled eggs, salad, fruit, soda, juice—whatever you would take on a picnic.

If it is a nice day, you might want to move everything outside to the lawn and pretend that you are having the picnic in a park.

Play games associated with picnics, like throwing a Frisbee; catch; foot races; and, if your yard is really big, badminton and volleyball.

❀　　　❀　　　❀　　　❀　　　❀

Let's Have More Fun! Draw or buy invitations in the shape of watermelon slices and include plastic ants in the envelope with the invitations.

Make the birthday cake in the shape of a watermelon using red and green icing and black licorice pieces or chocolate chips for the seeds.

If the party remains indoors, board games are fun. You can also try indoor Frisbee, a beanbag toss into a picnic basket, musical chairs, or "hot potato." To play the last game, have the children seated in a circle. They pass around a "hot" potato as music is playing. When the music stops, whoever holds the potato is out. Whoever is in charge of the music should have his or her back turned to the kids, in case of cries of favoritism.

Put wrapped packages of cakes, cookies, or crackers and small toys in a checkered napkin and tie with a bow for take-home favors.

❀ **Goosebumps Party** ❀

Cat Prindle
San Diego, California

Age Group: Seven to twelve years old
Invitations: Hand-drawn scary pictures
Special Theme Food: Scary pizza and cake
Decorations: Gory Goosebumps game board
Activities: A variety of gory games
Goodie Bag: Game prizes

❀   ❀   ❀   ❀   ❀

Here's What to Do: Since my daughter really loves the Goosebumps series of books—she has read all of them—we had a Goosebumps party for her seventh birthday.

The guests were invited to a scary stuff birthday party with an invitation showing a ghostly picture drawn by my daughter.

We made the whole house, inside and out, a giant Goosebumps game with a different gory activity in each room.

The children were divided into two groups, going in different directions. We covered a child's toy block with numbers one through four to use as a die for moving along a trail of squares made out of newspapers. Along the way, they would get cards saying things like "A vampire is trying to suck your blood, run back three spaces."

Pin the Heart on a Skeleton was played in a dimly lit bedroom. Other games were Throw the Snakes in the Snake Pit, Knock over the Skeleton Head with Beanbags, and Fish the Mystery Animal Out of the Bathtub. This mystery animal can be of your own design—remember, though, that rubber is super slimy under water!

In other games the children put their hands in a cauldron to fish out specially painted rocks, dug their hands through cold spaghetti in a tomb to find body parts, looked for Frankenstein's name on a tombstone in the backyard cemetery, crawled through haunted tunnels and counted the number of hanging spiders, and pulled Gummi worms off of a scary monster's head.

The kids got stickers each time they won an activity. All the guests pulled wrapped prizes out of a box, going in the order of how many stickers each person won. Prizes included Goosebumps books, puzzles, and scary things such as rubber insects, snakes, and skeletons.

For food, we had pizza with a scary face made on top. The cake was decorated with headstones cut out from cardboard with sayings on them, spiders and spider webs, and ghosts. We made a mummy out of a Ken doll and placed him on the cake, too. He never looked so good.

Our party was a lot of work to set up and do, but it was a real hit with all the boys and girls.

❁ Disney World at Home Party ❁

Evelyn Hester
Bartlett, Tennessee

Age Group: Six to ten years old
Invitations: Hand-delivered Mickey Mouse hats or paper Mickey Mouse ears
Special Theme Food: Snack bar service
Decorations: Disney World brochures and paraphernalia
Activities: Disney World–themed games
Goodie Bag: Disney World toys

❁   ❁   ❁   ❁   ❁

Here's What to Do: If you can't take all the kids to Disney World for the birthday party, bring Disney World to your home.

Get lots of brochures from Disney World to use as decorations on the walls. Set up signs around the house identifying different parts of the house as Fantasyland, Adventureland, Tomorrowland, Liberty Square, Mickey's Starland, and Frontierland.

At each location have some type of activity—such as word games, a maze, pictures to color, a simple craft to make—that matches the theme of that section of Disney World.

When serving the food, set it up like a refreshment stand at Disney World. Put the food in containers like the ones used at snack bars.

Play some background music from Disney movies.

Order by mail from the shops at Disney World some inexpensive items to give out as party favors.

❀　　　❀　　　❀　　　❀　　　❀

Let's Have More Fun! Use white paint pens to write invitations on black Mickey Mouse hats for hand-delivered invitations. If some invitations must be mailed, cut out Mickey Mouse ears from black construction paper and write information with white paint pens.

For one craft station have Mickey Mouse faces cut out of black felt. Have buttons, fabric scraps, fabric paint, and other materials for the children to decorate with. The children can also make their own magic wands out of cardboard stars that they can decorate with glitter, markers, and paint. Attach these to dowels, long pieces of cardboard, or popsicle sticks. And, of course, encourage the kids to "whistle while they work."

A Catered Affair

It might sound like it would cost a lot of money, but consider having your child's birthday party professionally catered if there will be a fair number of adults attending. You don't have to have fancy foods that you would find at an elaborate affair. Sometimes simple is best.

Hiring a local caterer can be a good deal for everyone. Once you total up all the costs of the food, beverages, plates, napkins, and so on, there might not be that much difference in cost between doing the party yourself and having it catered. Also, you will be spared all the time and effort preparing everything for the party.

—Hester Bianchi
Branford, Connecticut

Disney World items can be purchased at Disney stores in shopping malls or by mail from Disney World itself.

Mail Order/Guest Services
Walt Disney World Company
P.O. Box 10070
Lake Buena Vista, FL 32830-1000

Telephone: (407) 363-6200

❀ Fashion Show Party ❀

Dori Decker

Penbrook, Pennsylvania

Age Group: Four to twelve years old

Invitations: Hat cut out from light cardboard and decorated with a feather and sequins

Special Theme Food: Tea sandwiches, petit fours, and sparkling cider

Decorations: Pictures of high-fashion models

Activities: Dress-up runway fashion show

Goodie Bag: Fashion show outfits, photographs

❀　　❀　　❀　　❀　　❀

Here's What to Do: Fashion shows are always popular, so why not have a Fashion Show Birthday Party for girls? Not surprisingly, I don't think it would work too well for boys.

Have a lot of dress-up clothes, including scarves, hats, gloves, high-heel shoes, and jewelry for the girls to assemble different outfits. We got a lot of the dress-up stuff at secondhand stores, garage sales, and flea markets. Wash or clean everything before the party.

Set up a runway. Let each girl create an outfit. When they're ready, they each parade up and down while commentary is given. Have energetic music in the background. Give awards for numerous categories—most creative, most colorful, best coordination of accessories, and so on—so everyone wins a prize.

Have a camera ready, of course, and take plenty of pictures of everyone to send out later with the thank-you notes for the presents.

The girls get to take home the outfits they created for the fashion show.

❀　　❀　　❀　　❀　　❀

Let's Have More Fun! Cut out pictures of high-fashion models from magazines and hang them around the room.

Serve dainty tea sandwiches with the crusts cut off and petit fours. Sparkling cider with a maraschino cherry or a strawberry can be served in plastic champagne glasses during the fashion show to add a touch of real sophistication.

❀ Tisket, Tasket, Basket Party ❀

Alexandra Glover
Prichard, Alabama

Age Group: Four to nine years old
Invitations: Hand-delivered baskets
Special Theme Food: Food served in baskets, watermelon basket fruit cup, basket cake
Decorations: Hanging baskets, flowers, streamers
Activities: Basket games
Goodie Bag: Goodie baskets

❀   ❀   ❀   ❀   ❀

Here's What to Do: A Tisket, Tasket, Basket Party isn't hard to do, looks nice, and is lots of fun.

Hang baskets filled with flowers and streamers around the party room.

Fill a basket for each child with a sandwich, a box of raisins, a bag of chips, candies, a juice box, a napkin, and plastic utensils. Cut a watermelon into the shape of a basket and fill with fruit cup. Decorate the sides of the cake with brown frosting in a lattice pattern so it looks like a basket. Sprinkle all kinds of candies over the top of the cake to look like they are thrown inside the basket.

Play games using baskets. Have a contest with the kids competing to see how many balls they can toss into a basket in a given amount of time. We also had a relay race. The kids were divided into teams. Each child carried a basket filled with Ping-Pong balls and ran a specific distance and back to their team. They had to stop and retrieve any Ping-Pong balls that fell out of the basket. The winning team got prizes.

❀   ❀   ❀   ❀   ❀

Let's Have More Fun! Each guest receives a small hand-delivered basket with the invitation to the party tucked inside.

Instead of a goodie bag for the take-home favors, give out goodie baskets as the guests leave for home.

❀ Dinosaur Party ❀

Carol S. Howell
Asheville, North Carolina

Age Group: Six to twelve years old
Invitations: Large dinosaur eggs
Special Theme Food: Plastic eggs filled with dinosaur-shaped candies, dinosaur-era
birthday cake
Decorations: Painted stand-up dinosaurs
Activities: Painting dinosaurs, dinosaur egg hunt, picture taking
Goodie Bag: Dinosaur photo, dinosaur books, dinosaur toys

❀   ❀   ❀   ❀   ❀

Here's What to Do: The Dinosaur Party starts off with a dinosaur egg hunt with the children looking for plastic Easter eggs painted to look like real dinosaur eggs, which are hidden around the yard or in the house. Fill the eggs with dinosaur Gummi candies. Since the Gummi candies can melt, don't use them if your party is outdoors on a hot summer day. Substitute dinosaur toys or stickers if it's this kind of weather.

No Smoking, Please

It really should not even be necessary or a problem these days, but it is best to avoid any potential embarrassment for guests. It is quite possible that you will not know very well the parents who will be attending a birthday party in your home, and perhaps they have not visited you before. If you do not allow smoking in your home, be sure to place discreet NO SMOKING signs all around and on the front door to avoid any question about whether or not parents can light up while attending the party.

For our party we made four dinosaur cutouts from foam-core board and staked them out in the yard. The children enjoyed painting them with acrylic paint.

We made another cutout dinosaur, only this one had a hole where the face would be. We also set this up on the lawn so the children could poke their faces through and have their pictures taken. We used a Polaroid camera so each child could get a picture to take home as one of their party favors.

The birthday cake was shaped like a volcano with dinosaur candles and palm trees made from large pretzel sticks and frosting leaves.

Let's Have More Fun! For the invitations, cut out large egg-shaped pieces of gray cardboard. Draw cracks in the eggs and little feet coming out of the cracks. This dinosaur egg is hatching! Write the information on the other side.

There are many toy dinosaurs and books about dinosaurs available in stores, often at very reasonable prices, and they would make good take-home favors for a Dinosaur Party.

If you have a sandbox, hide toy dinosaur figures underneath the sand, and let the children enjoy an archaeological "dig."

For the painting, a supply of old T-shirts could come in very handy.

❀ Caribbean Party ❀

Susan Birchman
Poughkeepsie, New York

Age Group: Seven to twelve years old
Invitations: Gaily colored invitations sent along with a flower lei
Special Theme Food: Barbecue, tropical drinks, skewers of fresh tropical fruit, coconuts, pineapple upside-down cake
Decorations: Caribbean island theme posters, steel drum band music
Activities: Swimming, sand art, dancing
Goodie Bag: Sand art crafts, hula hoops

❀   ❀   ❀   ❀   ❀

Here's What to Do: A Caribbean Party was perfect for my daughter when she turned nine.

The decorations were bright island theme colors, and we also had posters of tropical places. We played a tape of steel drum music in the background to enhance the atmosphere.

After a dip in our pool and a barbecue, we enjoyed hula hoop contests with narrations of what their movements meant (for example, the sun shining and fish swimming), dancing "the macarena," and breaking a piñata shaped like an ocean liner.

To close out the party, we played Follow the Leader around the backyard, dancing with maracas to the song "Hot, Hot, Hot."

The hula hoops were taken home as a party favor.

    ❀   ❀   ❀   ❀   ❀

Let's Have More Fun! For invitations, cut out colorful pieces of paper in irregular shapes to resemble islands. Write the information in pen and send them in a large envelope with a toy flower lei.

For the birthday cake, have a pineapple upside-down cake for a sweet taste of the islands. Also serve nonalcoholic tropical drinks. Prepare skewers with pieces of fresh fruit like guava, papaya, mango, and pineapple. Break open whole coconuts and pass around pieces of the fresh coconut.

A fun activity is sand art. Have the children fill up small bottles with different layers of colored sand. The sand and bottles are available at most craft stores. And, of course, the completed sand art bottles would be another take-home party favor.

Eat, Drink, and Enjoy

Just because everyone says that they're so concerned about eating the right foods and avoiding the wrong foods, it doesn't mean that everything you serve at a birthday party must be nutritionally correct.

A birthday party is just a few hours out of a whole year, and it seems silly to worry about the "nutrition police" crashing into your home because the foods you are serving may be a little far from perfect.

A party is for enjoyment, for something you do differently from what you do every day.

—Francine Wood
Longmont, Colorado

❀ Wild West Party ❀

Laura Rogers
Bellflower, California

Age Group: Four to six years old
Invitations: Green cactus invitations
Special Theme Food: Prairie dogs, cattle chips, fruit on an arrow, cowboy cooler, western scene birthday cake
Decorations: Western items
Activities: Taking photographs, picture frames, tepee toss, stick pony race, bounce house
Goodie Bag: Framed picture

❀　　　❀　　　❀　　　❀　　　❀

Here's What to Do: To set the theme of our party we had western theme decorations, such as rope "lassos"; cowboy boots; and cutouts of cowboys, cowboy hats, and horses; paper goods; and cowboy-themed goodie bags. We also invited our guests to come dressed in keeping with the western theme.

We made a five-foot-high cardboard tepee surrounded by cardboard cactuses that we also made. As each guest arrived, their picture was taken with a Polaroid camera as they stood in the tepee doorway. The picture was kept aside for crafts later in the party.

Then all the guests got to play in an inflatable tepee bounce house that we rented for the day. After about a half hour in the bounce house, food was served.

We ate prairie dogs (store-bought mini–hot dogs in buns), cattle chips (plain potato chips), fruit on an arrow (chunks of fruit pieces on a wooden skewer), and cowboy cooler (fruit punch).

The bounce house was deflated while the food was served to avoid distractions and anyone getting sick by eating and jumping.

After lunch, while everyone's food settled, we did a craft project. Poster board had been cut ahead of time into picture frames that would fit a Polaroid picture. The children decorated their picture frames with scraps of paper and western stickers. Above the opening in the frame they wrote "Wanted" and below they wrote their own names. The Polaroid pictures taken upon arrival were taped in the opening of the frames so everyone had a personalized souvenir to take home.

After the wanted posters were completed, we played Tepee Toss (throwing homemade beanbags through the opening in the cardboard tepee), and held stick pony races with homemade stick ponies.

We had bales of straw for sitting on around the picnic tables and throughout the yard. Most feed supply stores carry bales of straw for a reasonable price, and they may give a refund of somewhat less than you paid if you return them in good condition. It's kind of like renting the bales.

After the games the bounce house was quickly reinflated; it only took about fifteen minutes.

Then came the cake, one layer decorated with a western scene including people, tepees, horses, canoes, and totem poles. Green sugar sprinkles were spread around to look like grass.

❀ ❀ ❀ ❀ ❀

Let's Have More Fun! Cut out invitations in cactus shapes from green construction paper and decorate them with black needles drawn in ink and maybe a blooming cactus flower.

Ouch!

Have a first aid kit or at least some basic first aid supplies handy, such as Band-Aids, antibiotic cream, and a "boo-boo bunny" for bumps. For any injury that requires any kind of treatment, no matter how trivial, it is wise to contact the child's parents and keep them informed of what happened and what you are doing.

❀ Backyard Seashore Party ❀

Raquel Brewer
Costa Mesa, California

Age Group: Three to six years old
Invitations: Plastic seashells
Special Theme Food: Blue Jell-O, fish-shaped crackers, chips in sand pails, sailboat sandwiches, theme cupcakes
Decorations: Wading pool paraphernalia
Activities: Noncompetitive poolside games
Goodie Bag: Decorated sun visors, game prizes

❀ ❀ ❀ ❀ ❀

Here's What to Do: For my daughter's third birthday, we held her first birthday party. While it was a first for her, it was also a first for me as hostess. Thus I spent a lot of time, thought, and energy planning this event to ensure perfection, and sure enough, it was perfect . . . a perfect nightmare!

The clown was "too scary," the blindfolds were "too scary," hitting a happy-faced clown piñata was too mean, and there were too many children!

It has been a few years now since that unforgettable day, and at the time I thought I'd never again plan another party for three-year-olds. But this month my son turned three and once again I found myself planning. However, this time I tried to think three-year-old style, small and simple. The results were perfect, period.

I used "backyard beach" as a theme for activities, food, and everything else. There were no games, just "everyone wins" activities like fishing for prizes, digging for treasures (coins, shells) in a sandbox, decorating sun visors, tattoo application (temporary, of course), beach ball bouncing, bubble popping, and a wading pool. (The wading pool proved to be a little more effort than I had hoped, but the children enjoyed it. You'll definitely want extra parental supervision around the pool.) I also provided a child-friendly lunch with my son's favorite, peanut butter and honey, but with a creative twist. I spread the peanut butter and honey on top of half a hot dog bun. Then I wove a wooden skewer through a triangle-shaped piece of fruit leather. I stuck the "sail" in the center of the hot dog bun, so it looked like a sailboat.

I also served chips out of sand buckets, fish-shaped crackers, blue Jell-O with candy fish on top, finger fruits, veggies, and water. For the finale I frosted cupcakes with blue frosting to resemble water and then placed a small rubber boat on top of each one.

The party was a fun, creative outlet for me, and my son loved it, which, lest we forget, is the real reason for the party. This party will definitely "sail" smoothly.

❀　　　❀　　　❀　　　❀　　　❀

Let's Have More Fun! You can get plastic seashells for the invitations at most party goods stores. Write all the information on them with a nonsmearing felt tip pen. Mail them in a padded envelope so they will not break.

Plan Ahead

If you are going to have a coordinated theme for the party, choose one with your child well in advance of the date of the party. You then can start gathering all the things you need without any pressure and without last-minute rushes for some special decorations or favors that you just have to have.

3

Sure-to-Please Party Foods

❀   ❀   ❀   ❀   ❀   ❀   ❀

Before the Cake and Ice Cream

Although all the children want cake and ice cream—the traditional and essential treats for almost every party—they are hungry and growing people who need more to eat than desserts for an afternoon of excitement, activities, and fun.

There are many different things you can serve, depending upon your own preferences; what is popular in your area; the ages of the guests; and, of course, your son's or daughter's own tastes.

Here, though, to get you started planning a party menu, is a selection of foods that will make everyone happy . . . and full:

No Food Surprises

Sometimes the food served at birthday parties for children will be just cake, cookies, ice cream, and drinks. Other times there will be a complete selection of foods from peanut butter and jelly sandwiches to cold cuts, salads, vegetable platters, and fruits along with the usual party favorites.

In order to let parents know what their children will be offered—as well as the parents who are attending the party—it is helpful to mention on the invitation if a complete meal will be served or only desserts.

If you do not want to include the refreshments on the invitation, a telephone call to the parents informing them of what will be served would provide the same information.

- pizza
- hot dogs
- little hot dogs in crescent rolls (pigs in blankets)
- hamburgers on rolls
- minihamburgers on dinner rolls

- chicken nuggets
- peanut butter and jelly sandwiches
- cream cheese and jelly sandwiches
- cheese and cold cuts on a platter
- small cold cuts sandwiches
- hard-boiled eggs

- franks and beans
- spaghetti and meatballs
- lasagna
- shish kebabs
- fried chicken
- chicken wings
- spare ribs
- barbecue beef on rolls
- sausage and peppers
- pork roll sandwiches
- cheese steak sandwiches
- submarine sandwiches
- grilled cheese sandwiches
- macaroni and cheese
- popcorn shrimp
- corn on the cob
- baked potatoes with toppings
- french fried potatoes
- cheese fondue

- tacos
- burritos
- enchiladas
- mild chili
- egg rolls
- fried wontons
- fried potato puffs
- potato skins
- nachos with melted cheese
- mozzarella sticks
- fried onion rings
- minibagels
- bread sticks
- garlic bread
- carrot sticks
- cut-up fruit pieces
- chips
- olives
- pickles

❀ A Variety of Cake Decorations ❀

There are so many different things that can be used to decorate a birthday cake.

Any list of what to put on a cake is, well, incomplete, since everyone can always think of many more eatable, decorative treats. You are limited only by your own imagination and artistic talents.

Here, though, is a list to get you started on decorations that are as good as treats to eat as they are to look at:

- red and black licorice strings
- red and black licorice pieces
- small cinnamon heart-shaped candies
- chocolate wafer cookies
- vanilla wafer cookies
- gumdrops of all sizes
- chocolate shavings
- sprinkles

- nonpareils of all sizes
- thin pretzel sticks
- flaked coconut; plain, toasted, and tinted with food coloring
- chocolate chips
- mint chocolate chips
- butterscotch chips
- vanilla chips
- peanut butter chips

- M&M's candies; regular-size and mini-size, regular and peanut
- colored sugar crystals
- lollipops
- marshmallows; regular-size and mini-size
- chocolate-covered mint patties
- chocolate kisses
- Life Savers candies
- small silver candy balls (dragées)
- candy confetti in various shapes
- candied fruit
- Good & Plenty candies
- jelly beans; regular-size and mini-size
- shelled peanuts and other nuts
- Tic Tac candies
- chocolate-covered malted milk balls
- chocolate-covered raisins
- chocolate-covered peanuts
- green mint candy gumdrop leaves
- orange candy gumdrop slices
- Gummi bear candies
- mini-size cookies
- red and white round, hard peppermint candies
- peppermint stick candies
- crushed cookie crumbs
- orange slices
- grapes
- strawberries
- kiwi slices
- melon balls
- pineapple pieces
- Jujyfruits candies
- Dots candies
- Pez candies

Food for All

This hint often gets overlooked in the preparty planning: be sure to have appropriate food and beverages for the *parents* if they will be staying at your party along with their children. Not all adults like kid food, and every person who comes to your home—adults as well as children—deserves the best of your hospitality.

—Rita Compton
Haysville, Kansas

Traditional White Cake

2½ cups flour

3 teaspoons baking powder

½ teaspoon salt

1½ cups sugar

½ cup shortening

1 cup milk

1½ teaspoons vanilla extract

2 eggs

Preheat oven to 350°F.

Sift flour, baking powder, and salt. Set aside.

Cream sugar and shortening. Add flour, ¾ cup of the milk, and vanilla extract, beating until smooth. Add eggs and remaining ¼ cup of the milk, mixing together well.

Pour batter into two well-greased 9-inch cake pans or one well-greased 9-inch-by-13-inch pan.

Bake for 30 to 35 minutes, or until a toothpick inserted into the center of the cake comes out clean.

Remove from oven, let cool for ten minutes, and then remove cake from pans.

Let cool completely before covering with frosting.

Chocolate Devil's Food Delight Cake

1¾ cups flour

1 teaspoon baking soda

½ teaspoon salt

1⅓ cups sugar

½ cup butter or margarine

1 cup milk

1½ teaspoons vanilla extract

2 eggs

3 ounces unsweetened
chocolate, melted

Preheat oven to 350°F.

Sift flour, baking soda, and salt. Set aside.

Cream sugar and butter and add flour mixture. Stir in milk and vanilla extract. Beat for two minutes on medium speed of electric mixer. Add eggs and melted chocolate. Beat two minutes more until batter is thoroughly mixed.

Pour batter into two well-greased 9-inch layer cake pans and bake for 30 to 35 minutes, or until a toothpick inserted into the center of the cake comes out clean.

The cake can also be made in one well-greased 9-inch-by-13-inch pan and baked for 35 to 40 minutes.

Remove from oven and let cool for ten minutes. Remove cake from pan.

Let cool completely before covering with frosting.

Jam Cake

2½ cups sifted flour

1 teaspoon ground cinnamon

1 teaspoon baking soda

¼ teaspoon ground allspice

¼ teaspoon ground nutmeg

¾ cup butter or margarine, softened

1 cup sugar

3 eggs

1 cup seedless raspberry or blackberry preserves

¾ cup buttermilk

2 tablespoons apple juice

Preheat oven to 350°F.

Sift together flour, cinnamon, baking soda, allspice, and nutmeg. Set aside.

Beat together butter, sugar, and eggs until light and fluffy. Stir in raspberry preserves. Stir in flour mixture alternately with buttermilk and apple juice until batter is smooth.

Spoon batter into two greased and floured 8-inch layer cake pans.

Bake for 30 to 35 minutes, or until top of cake springs back lightly pressed with fingertips.

Remove from oven and cool on wire racks for ten minutes before removing from pan.

Let cool completely before covering with frosting.

Chocolate Surprise Cupcakes

8 ounces cream cheese, softened

I egg

1⅓ cups plus 2 tablespoons sugar

dash of salt

I cup chocolate chips

1½ cups flour

¼ cup unsweetened cocoa powder

I teaspoon baking soda

I cup water

⅓ cup vegetable oil

I tablespoon vinegar

I teaspoon vanilla extract

½ cup ground pecans

Preheat oven to 350°F.

Beat cream cheese. Add egg, ⅓ cup of the sugar, and salt. Add chocolate chips. Set aside.

Sift together flour, 1 cup of the sugar, cocoa powder, and baking soda. Set aside.

Combine water, vegetable oil, vinegar, and vanilla extract. Beat until well mixed. Add to flour mixture.

Spoon cocoa mixture into paper-lined cupcake tins, filling ⅓ of the cupcake papers. Spoon cream cheese and chocolate chip mixture over top, filling papers.

Combine the remaining 2 tablespoons of sugar and the ground pecan. Sprinkle over top of cupcakes.

Bake for 30 to 35 minutes, or until a toothpick inserted into the center of a cupcake comes out clean.

Remove from oven and let cool.

Cream Cheese Icing

3 ounces cream cheese,
softened

1 tablespoon warm milk

2½ cups confectioners' sugar

1 teaspoon vanilla extract

Beat together cream cheese and milk until smooth. Gradually add confectioners' sugar and beat until creamy. Add in vanilla extract, mixing until smooth.

Spread on any cooled cake.

Chocolate Peppermint Icing

⅓ cup butter or margarine, softened

2 ounces unsweetened chocolate, melted

dash of salt

3 cups confectioners' sugar

¼ cup milk

1 teaspoon peppermint extract

Cream butter, chocolate, and salt. Add 1 cup of the confectioners' sugar, mixing until light and fluffy. Alternately add remaining 2 cups of confectioners' sugar and milk, beating well. Add peppermint extract and continue beating until icing is very smooth.

Spread on any cooled cake.

Fluffy White Frosting

2 egg whites

1½ cups sugar

dash of salt

½ cup water

1 tablespoon light corn syrup

1½ teaspoons vanilla extract

Combine egg whites, sugar, salt, water, and corn syrup. Place mixture in the top of a double boiler and heat over boiling water, beating constantly with a rotary beater on high speed for about seven minutes or until frosting stands in stiff peaks. Add vanilla extract, beating well.

Remove from heat and let cool.

Spread on any cooled cake.

Cream Cheese Chocolate Frosting

3 ounces cream cheese,
softened

¼ cup milk

2 ounces unsweetened
chocolate, melted

2½ cups confectioners' sugar

1 teaspoon vanilla extract

dash of salt

Beat cream cheese until smooth. Add milk, melted chocolate, confectioners' sugar, vanilla extract, and salt, beating until smooth.

Spread on any cooled cake.

Buttercream Frosting

¼ cup butter or margarine

2 cups confectioners' sugar

¼ cup milk

1 teaspoon vanilla extract

Cream butter and confectioners' sugar. Add milk and vanilla extract, mixing together until smooth.

Spread on any cooled cake.

Hot Fudge Sauce

1 cup sugar

1 cup milk

2 tablespoons flour

2 tablespoons unsweetened
   cocoa powder

1 teaspoon vanilla extract

2 tablespoons butter or
   margarine

Place all the ingredients in a heavy saucepan and cook over medium heat, stirring constantly, until sauce is thoroughly mixed. Continue stirring until sauce has thickened, about four to five minutes.

Quick Caramel Sauce

2 cups butterscotch chips

½ cup light corn syrup

2 tablespoons water

1 tablespoon vegetable oil

Place all the ingredients in a heavy saucepan and cook over medium heat, stirring constantly until butterscotch chips dissolve. Continue stirring until sauce is completely mixed and smooth.

Ice-Cream Pie

1 cup Grape-Nuts cereal, finely
   ground
3 to 4 tablespoons Quick
   Caramel Sauce (see page 148)

Pie Crust

Mix together Grape-Nuts cereal and caramel syrup and then press mixture onto the bottom and up the sides of an 8-inch pie pan.

½ gallon ice cream or frozen
   yogurt, flavor of your choice

Pie Filling

Allow ice cream to soften slightly. When spreadable with a spatula, fill pie crust with ice cream.

Peanut Butter Chocolate Topping

⅓ cup chocolate syrup

⅓ cup chunky peanut butter

⅓ cup caramel syrup

Mix together chocolate syrup, peanut butter, and caramel syrup. Pour mixture over ice-cream pie.

Chill pie in freezer until solid.

Take pie from freezer and let stand at room temperature for fifteen minutes before serving.

The guests are gone,
  The house is a mess,
But everyone is happy,
  The party was a success.

❀ Index ❀